Without Method

Christine Sayre

BookLeaf Publishing

India | USA | UK

Presentation by *BookLeaf Publishing*

Web: www.bookleafpub.com

E-mail: info@bookleafpub.com

ISBN: 9789363311473

First edition 2024

To those who have touched my life in ways seen and unseen, this book is dedicated to you. The presence, support, and love have shaped this journey and fueled my creativity. May these words serve as a testament to the impact you have had on my life, even if you did not know the extent of it. With heartfelt gratitude and admiration, this book is dedicated to each of you.

ACKNOWLEDGEMENT

Shout-out to the people who started it all, my parents Brandi and Bobby, I love you both and thank you for always being there for me. To my siblings, Shane, Michael, Noelani & Abraham. You guys are the best thing since margaritas and tacos! Thanks for being my built-in friends and I love you to death.

To all the people who have come and gone, thanks for being a part of my journey. Even to those who may have hurt me, I appreciate the growth and strength that arose from those experiences. Your presence, in whatever form it took, has shaped me in ways I am grateful for.

.

PREFACE

In *Without Method*, I invite you to dive into a collection of poems that express the unpredictable waves of life, each verse crafted in free verse as a tribute to the untamed beauty of existence. As a girl hailing from Cleveland with a deep-seated dream of sharing my words with the world, this collection is a culmination of my innermost thoughts, feelings and some experiences.

In these pages, you'll read about random thoughts coming from the dead of night when lying in bed, raw honesty, betrayal, reflection and my worldly experience with people who I care about. All while seeking solace within these experiences because not all were positive.

I hope that the words in this book resonate with you, evoke emotions, and spark contemplation about your own experiences and perceptions. May *Without Method* serves as a reminder that while things may start unstructured, they have a way of transforming into something beautiful and meaningful in their own time.
Just take my word for it, this book proves it.

Warm regards,
Chrissy Ann

From Cleveland with words

In the heart of Cleveland, a dream took flight,
A girl with a pen, reaching for the light.
Longing to write, through struggles and tears,
Afraid of failure, of doubts and fears.

But as time went on, she found her way,
Learning from setbacks, growing each day.
Who cares about judgment, from those who
don't see,
Her dream was hers, to become and be.

Inspiration found in the everyday grind,
In moments of hope, in moments kind.
She absorbed it all, with a heart wide open,
Letting her words flow, her passion unbroken.

Regardless of readers, regardless of fame,
She wrote for herself, staking her claim.
Seeing her name on the cover, a dream coming true,
A girl from Cleveland, writing just for you.

So live in the moment, embrace what you find,
Let your words flow, leaving doubt behind.
Write about the world, about lessons learned,
For in your words, a story will churn.

Growing pains

As children, we couldn't wait to be grown,
To break free from rules and have minds of our
own.
But as we grow older, we soon realize,
That adulthood can come with its own set of
cries.
The carefree days of youth, they slip away,
Replaced by duties we face every day.
No more playing without a single thought,
Our worries and fears can't be forgotten.

Yet in the whirlwind of change and time,
We learn to savor each mountain we climb.
Life will never stay the same,
And that's not always a burden or a blame.
With years come wisdom, a deeper insight,
An understanding that feels just right.
So let's seize this moment, this very now,

Growth is a journey, but we'll learn somehow.
To navigate the curves and bends,
To endure the storms and still be friends.

We hold onto memories of our past,
But embrace the present, it goes by fast.
Life is a gift, a treasure so grand,
Growing up is part of the plan.
Let's treasure the moments we leave behind,
But live in the now, in the present we find.

Cinnamon & Pear

In the soft scent of Cinnamon & Pear,
A love story begins, so radiant and rare.
Two souls entwined, perfect in each other's eyes,
Promises made under clear blue skies.

So it began, a bond formed on a bed of lies,
Deception hidden behind loving eyes.

Bound by commitment with another
yet behaving like a bachelor,
With no regard for consequences, causing a
disaster.

My time stolen, bit by bit
A digital puppeteer Disguised as her
Pulling at my heartstrings to lure me back.
Those moments stolen are irretrievable.

I thought I knew you, but you were a stranger
wearing a mask of affection, pretending to care
your words were empty,
your touch a lie
leaving me shattered,
wondering why.

And finally..
Our bond is untangled
Forgiveness wanes and scars remain.
The journey ahead, uncertain yet bright,
With lessons learned through tough nights
Cinnamon & Pear, a love thought to be true.
A duo that will never again renew.

Bee Hive

Did you know a bee hive has one Queen bee?
She is a central figure in her community.
The queen bee is responsible for the
reproduction, organization and her presence is
vital for the hive to thrive.

The women in my life are like Queen Bees,
Central figures who love with
tenderness and toughness.

These beautiful souls
will lend a helping hand where they can, wipe
your tears away and pick you up because we
aren't built to cry & whine for long.

Prayers are said night and day and these
beautiful women might hear back from God
Himself to let them know all is well.
They have that divine connection.

This sisterhood of women stood tall and some
stood short with grace and sass.
You better watch your ass,
most of them would say.
With soft eyes they would open their arms and
hug tightly. The world never felt so safe in these
moments.

Fearless and unapologetic style of humor set
them apart and added a sense of excitement to
our gatherings.

With each one a queen in her own right
And with some who are no longer with us
anymore I still feel their presence.
Their laughter is still fresh in my memory.

I can still smell their cigarettes like they exhaled
in front of me.
A certain song comes on and I am brought back
to the moment they're singing in the kitchen
while cooking.

It's a real tear jerker.

Queen Bees still reign in my hive.
With the same sass, unity, with beauty and
brains, and that will forever remain
I'm proud to be a part of this sisterhood.

In their footsteps we'll follow, and the ones after
us will walk too
a legacy that is proudly ours to bear.

Pele

Like a Volcano, I am patient
Slow to anger, slow to react
But when the pressure builds
And the lava starts to flow
There is no stopping the eruption.

Strawberries

In solitude, with a coffee cup in hand,
I seek solace from the chaos outside.
But in the quiet, my heart longs for more,
A touch, a laugh, a hand to hold.

Balancing independence and desire,
I navigate the complexities of life.
Seeking solace in solitude's embrace,
While open to the possibility of love's grace.

From Paradise to Dystopia

In the land of dreams, I find myself in Hawaii,
Walking through a dense forest under a vast sky.
Greenery surrounds me, birds singing in the air,
Flowers blooming everywhere, beyond compare.

I reach the ocean, its waters crystal blue,
I dive in, feeling free, my spirit renewed.
Swimming, frolicking, in pure bliss I reside,
In this paradise, where all my troubles subside.

But then I awaken, back in the bustling city,
Sirens wailing, people talking, oh what a pity.
I call this dream "Falling Asleep in Hawaii,
Waking Up in Cleveland," a bittersweet fantasy.

Yearning for that paradise, where I felt so alive,
I hold onto the memory, letting out a long sigh.
Though it's not my reality right now, I'll cherish
it all the same,
And keep dreaming of Hawaii, where my heart
claims.

Going through the motions

In the hustle and bustle of life, my parents
Who were just kids
Figuring it out with a child of their own.

Nearly raised on the shores of Hawaii.
But decisions shifted and hearts broke,
Leaving behind what almost could have been,
A different life for us all.

In a place of bars and guards, my father was
confined. Despite the chaos, his love for us
never waned, Wisdom gained in solitude, body
and mind, A protector, a provider, his love
unrestrained.

From his fiery days to his peaceful nights,
Rushing to help, always ready to defend,
With jokes and love, his inner light shines
bright,
A father who'll stand by, until the very end.

My mother, a warrior in her own right,
In my early years, her presence was fleeting,
But as I grew, she became my guiding light,
A best friend, a confidante, never retreating,
Overcoming fears together through every fight.

Through ups and downs, they both learned to
mend,
Raising me separately yet with love and
toughness so true,
I wouldn't trade them for the world, my creators,
For their love, their support, in all that I do.

Grateful for their presence, for their care,
For the struggles and joys, the memories bright,
In this journey of life, they are always there,
My parents, my anchors, my guiding light.
For this, it has shaped me for who I am meant to
be.

4 legged Best Friend

Lucy Woocy, my mini poodle with fur golden
like the sun,
Her big ol' beady eyes watching me every
second of the day.
I love her for many reasons,
From her zany, ready to play all the time
attitude,
To knowing when it's bedtime or
The moment she barks at me because Larry
wants back in.
She alone brings so much light and laughter in
this journey I'm on, I'm grateful.
In Lucy's presence, my heart finds peace.

Breath of fresh air

I catch myself staring at you
Lost in thoughts of what could be
My heart racing and my mind spinning
Do you feel it too, or am I just a fool?

I imagine the words slipping from my lips
"I love you" spoken with trembling breath
Will you feel the same, or will I be left
With my heart on the line, vulnerable and
exposed?

Am I a fool for falling for you too soon?
Or am I a psychic, seeing the future unfold
Either way, I can't deny the truth
That I like you a lot, and one day, I may love
you.

A Part of Me

Earth.
Our wise and ancient mother.
Who is nurturing and life-giving
A force to be respected and admired, even if she
can be brutal at times.
This world is a part of me as I'm a part of it.
But my world?
My world that is the center of my being and
is much smaller.
It holds the ones who I love deeply,
Laugh out loud with,
the ones I'll debate with
whose shoulder I cry on
The ones I Travel the world with
cook together because we love food.
And shoot the shit with.

I pray I grow old with those who are a part of
my world.
And guess who else is a part of this?
The one who holds this very book in their hands.
because without any of you, this book would
gather dust and fade.

Nons

In her, youth's gentle grace,
Big heart beats with love so true,
Proud she's my sister.

SMS

Marches to his own beat,
Handy with tools, heart of gold,
Brother's light shines bright.

MAC jr

Eyes like frozen seas,
Dependable and steadfast,
Brother, my anchor.

Toads

Once a baby boy,
Now a man who brings me smiles,
Proud of who you are.

Cutting the rope.

For years,
The weight of hurt
the weight of anger
the weight of resentment,
weighs a heavy burden on our shoulders.
We try to forgive but it's hard to forget.
Then one day you hear a story that birthed a
humbling realization.
You don't have to keep carrying this weight.
Because it's a journey we're all on and some
don't even know it
Until one day..
our hearts, our minds
begin to open up

to the process of letting go.
Release the pain
And become free.
Ahhh you feel that weight leave your body yet?
Work on it.
Because I've learned that
Forgiveness is possible when it seems
impossible.

The OBE Chronicles

I periodically find my head not connected to my body,
Standing still, yet lost in thought, taking up space. I'm supposed to be paying attention to what's in front of me,
But my mind is elsewhere, wandering, free to be.

Please, allow me to show you a little something...
I'm drawn to the unknown, the mysteries of the world,
Exploring ideologies, the afterlife, and the divine. I dissect my spiritual experiences, trying to make sense of the dreams that haunt me, and the messages that have been sent.

What are these nudges and signs?
Why me, of all people, do I receive them?
The energy I pour into these explorations is endless, A hunger that can't be sated, a quest that's relentless.

But oh, the frustration that comes with this wandering mind, when I'm stuck in thought, and the world leaves me behind.

Ahhh, I gotta snap out of it, before I'm left behind, people are waiting, and I'm stuck in my own mind.

BEGIN

As we close this book, I want to leave you with a thought, That the journey doesn't have to end here, it's just a pause. For every ending is a new beginning, and every beginning is a new chance to explore, find your purpose, and elevate your craft, because the world needs new voices, and new hearts that desire.